CW00520077

Unethical Life Pro Tips

An Unethical Life Pro Tip is a tip that improves your life often at the expense of others.

Due to their nature, do not actually follow any of these tips. These tips are simply for entertainment value and many are not legal.

I would like to thank
my wife only because by
doing so I will profit and
if I don't I will suffer.

Table of Contents

Section 1: Workplace Hijinks

Tip 1: False Credentials

Applying for a new job without a college degree?

Pretend that you graduated from a decent university; companies rarely fact-check your resumé.

If they do check, the only consequence is that you don't get hired.

Tip 2: The Resumé Hack

Facing some difficulty in securing a job interview?

Type in some keywords – in white and the smallest possible font size so as to be invisible to the human eye – from the relevant job posting in the footer of your resumé.

If the HR department is using keyword scanning software to narrow down applications, you'll definitely make the shortlist.

Tip 3: Impression Management

Looking forward to a crucial job interview?

Have a few of your friends apply for the same position.

After they've each given a disastrous or lackluster interview, the odds of getting hired will be in your favor.

Tip 4: Shrewd Negotiator

Negotiating your salary with a new employer?

Tell them that you earn more than you actually do at your current position – and that you're happy to "stay at your current salary".

They will usually give you a raise anyway – without the need for a potentially stressful negotiation.

Tip 5: Set Yourself Up for Success

Did you just start a new job?

Never give them your 100% on your first few days. By putting in 75% on most days, you can occasionally get away with 50% of effort with the assumption that you're having a bad day.

Step it up to 100% as you get closer to your performance evaluation and/or annual review to boost your chances of getting a raise or bigger bonus.

Tip 6: All My Grandparents are Alive

Are you tired of rationing out your annual leave days?

Whenever you start a new job, make sure you have four valid excuses for missing work.

Keep track of your fictional hospital visits, medical emergencies, and funerals – and enjoy all your extra days off!

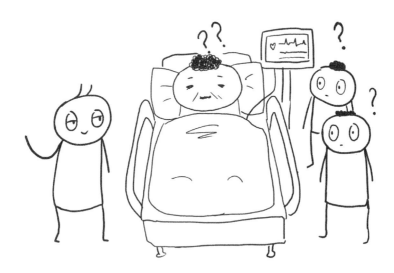

Tip 7: It's All in the Timing

Does your office layout allow you to enter without being noticed by your colleagues?

If so, avoid greeting them immediately when you enter.

When you're late to work, they will just assume that you haven't come over to greet them just yet.

Tip 8: Napping at Work

Did the boss catch you sleeping at work?

Tell him your drowsiness is an after-effect from donating blood the previous day.

Enjoy your shame-free nap.

Note: This will be more convincing with a bandage on your arm. If possible, apply one (discreetly) before falling asleep.

Tip 9: Quick Fix

Did a digital dinosaur just ask you to fix his or her laggy computer in the office?

Notch up their cursor speed to the maximum setting.

They will immediately notice their "fixed" computer and shower you with gratitude.

Note: This also works with smartphones – notching up the animation speed can make a phone feel brand new.

Tip 10: Slacking Off

Bored at work but worried about your eagled-eyed boss?

Copy + paste the text content of your favorite articles into your email.

Read on and keep boredom at bay!

Tip 11: Sting Like a Bee

Wish you could get even with a hateful boss?

Glue a dead wasp to the palm of your hand. Now you have an excuse to hit him on the back of the head as hard as you can.

Savor the sweetness of revenge.

Tip 12: Employee of the Year

Do you work in retail or customer service and wish to fast-track your way to a promotion or a hefty bonus?

Use a fake email address to send in glowing customer reviews of yourself every now and then.

Praise without merit goes a long way.

 Thanks to Frank, my life is saved and I am spending life savings on Restaurant gift cards!

Tip 13: Contagion

Want more legitimate excuses to skip work?

Keep note of when your colleagues are calling in sick. Wait a few days, and then claim that you've caught the flu bug of the season from them.

Getting paid while working less keeps the doctor at bay.

Tip 14: Feinting Spell

Feeling tired at work?

Take a nap on the floor in a random location.

Enjoy the extra sympathy and concern from your colleagues who will assume that you fainted. You might even get the rest of the day off!

Tip 15: Interminable Meetings

Hopelessly bored of a never-ending meeting?

Stand up abruptly and leave the room in a hurry while staring intently at your phone.

Your boss and colleagues will assume that something urgent has happened. Think of a credible story as you enjoy your downtime.

Tip 16: False Positives

Expecting a drug test at work?

Prepare a batch of THC-laced cookies or brownies for your colleagues.

HR can't possibly fire *everyone* who tests positive.

Tip 17: Revenge Hotline

Is there a colleague or superior that you hate?

Keep his or her business card in your glove compartment.

If you ever hit a parked vehicle by accident, write "Sorry!" on the back and leave it under the wiper.

Note: If you are accused of identity fraud, just claim that you wrote your name on the wrong card in the heat of the moment.

Don't want to frame someone you know? Leave $5 and a note claiming that you're five years old and that you fell down from your bike.

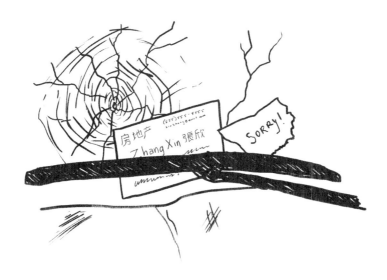

Tip 18: Zoning Out

Not in the mood to work today?

Reserve the meeting room and play some lo-fi jazz music from your phone.

Tell everyone who asks that you're stuck on hold and pretend to be frustrated.

Tip 19: Remote Productivity

Do you occasionally work remotely?

Use the "send at a specific time" feature to strategize on the timing of your emails.

Your boss will have the impression that you're working throughout the day even when you're slacking off.

Tip 20: Doctor's Note

Want to get out of work for a few days?

Pretend that you have a cold or diarrhea and tell your doctor that you work in the food industry.

Enjoy a few extra days off!

Tip 21: Plagiarism Checker

Need to complete some academic writing with minimal effort?

Copy and paste the relevant paragraphs from the Spanish version of Wikipedia (es.wikipedia. org) into Google Translate.

Submit your work without getting flagged for plagiarism.

Tip 22: A Convincing Lie

Want less responsibilities at work?

Fake a physical injury which won't allow for physical effort.

Be sure to keep up appearances even when no one is watching you.

This way, even undetected observers or security cameras won't blow your cover.

Tip 23: Retail Wars

Do you own a business that's competing against Walmart?

Spread unionization propaganda (flyers, emails, etc.) to all its employees.

Once they get laid off, you can hire the best of them and boost your sales as Walmart becomes temporarily "closed for renovations".

Tip 24: Covert Reform

Feeling powerless to affect change in your workplace?

When a colleague gets fired or quits, be sure to leave a Glassdoor review that outlines the policy changes you'd like to see.

Things will get better with some time and patience.

Section 2: Frugal Living

Tip 25: Student Discount

Don't want to give up your college student discounts?

Pretend that you've lost your student ID during your last year of college.

You get an additional four years of discounts once the expiration date is reset.

Tip 26: Free Stock Images

Don't want to pay for a stock photo?

You can find a watermark-free version by doing a reverse image search on the photo.

If a media company has already purchased it for use in an article, you can save a watermark-free version with just a few clicks.

Tip 27: The Laundry Pirate

Tired of saving all those coins for laundry day?

Take note of the model of the washer and/or dryer in your building. Order the relevant key on eBay and use it to access the control panel.

Start the cycle without any coins!

Note: Did a fellow resident become suspicious? Tell him or her that you moonlight as a laundry maintenance technician.

Tip 28: More for Less

Want fancy sports tickets without burning a hole in your wallet?

Purchase the cheapest tickets available for your favorite sporting event.

Once you get into the stadium, locate the best unsold seats on Ticketmaster and Stubhub. Relocate accordingly.

Note: If there is a ticket checker in the way, pretend that you belong there. If they insist on seeing your ticket, you might get away with a (discreet) bribe.

Tip 29: Maxing Out

Are you working as a cashier for a big grocery store?

When a customer makes a purchase without a rewards or loyalty card, swipe your personal card instead.

Make the most of all the additional points!

Note: To minimize suspicion, you might want to use several cards to rack up points. You could also save your secret swipes for larger purchases.

Tip 30: I Scream for Ice Cream

Want more ice cream without paying extra?

When you order your ice cream, always get a single scoop first. Once the server is done, tell him or her you've changed your mind and you now want a double scoop.

Now you get to enjoy two full-sized scoops!

Note: You might want to keep some tissues handy since spillage is likely.

Tip 31: The Free Delivery Hack

Are you annoyed that your preferred online store has a high purchase threshold for free deliveries?

Top up your order with an online gift card and cash it in during your next purchase. Then keep on repeating!

Enjoy free shipping without unnecessary spending.

Note: this means that you're effectively paying the store an advance on your next purchase.

Tip 32: Hazard-free Payment Information

Want to enjoy a free trial without committing your payment information?

Sign up for an account on the Spanish or Belgium PayPal – neither requires you to disclose your credit card information.

Secure all the free trials you want without worrying about cancelling or getting charged.

Note: Privacy.com offers a disposable credit card service just for this.

Tip 33: Cutting Out the Middleman

Hoping to buy a second-hand video game console or tablet during the holiday season?

Stand and wait outside a GameStop and keep an eye out for someone who is planning to trade in what you're looking for.

Offer them slightly more than what GameStop will give them. Enjoy the bargain price!

Tip 34: Standard Voucher

Ready to checkout online but you don't have any coupons or vouchers to use?

Try using a selection of common codes and see which one applies: "military", "sorry", "admin", "test", "free" etc.

Watch your checkout balance get reduced.

Note: You might need to experiment with some word and number combinations, e.g. "sorry20" or "sorry30".

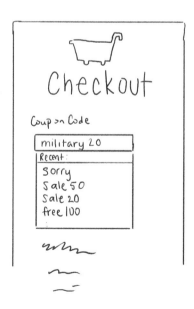

Tip 35: Budget Caffeine

Do the cafes on your college campus use a punch card reward system?

Look for the same hole-puncher design that they use online and buy it.

Get a bunch of reward cards and punch your way to an unlimited supply of free coffee.

Tip 36: Student Discount

Planning a Euro trip from outside the EU?

Create a fake student ID from your home country.

Enjoy all the discounts and student concessions (e.g. at museums) since they won't have a way of verifying your enrolment.

Tip 37: Lost and Found

Would you like a free phone or some spare cash?

Volunteer to clean-up after a large concert or music festival.

Pocket everything that's worth your while.

Tip 38: Peer-to-Peer

Are you planning to buy some used goods via a marketplace like OfferUp or Craigslist?

Create several accounts and use the others to spam the seller with insultingly low offers.

You'll be in a better position to convince the buyer that your (honest) offer is the best one.

Tip 39: Sentimental Value

Ready to propose?

Instead of spending a fortune on a flashy new wedding ring, purchase an old one from a pawn shop.

Tell your girlfriend that it was your grandmother's.

Tip 40: Unlimited Free Trials

Looking for a convenient way to sign up for multiple free trial sessions?

Purchase a domain name from Google Domains and establish a "catch-all" for emails. This means that any email address which ends with "@yourdomain.com" will be forwarded to your main email account.

Simply invent a new email address with your domain name whenever you want to sign up for another free trial.

catlover123 @ frank.com
doglover 123 @ frank.com
email 1 @ frank.com
email 2 @ frank.com
email 3 @ frank.com
cool guy 1 @ frank.com
coolerguy @ frank.com

Tip 41: Bad Santa

Are you kids young enough to believe in Santa?

Leave them with a bag of coal for Christmas and tell them that poor Santa must have made a mistake.

Buy them their gifts during the post-Christmas sales and earn their unmitigated adoration.

Tip 42: Tax Avoidance

Do you wish to give someone over $15,000 in the US?

Avoid the gift tax by having them sue you for personal injury.

"Settle" with them out of court and enjoy the tax-free transaction.

Section 3:
Tinder Mischief

Tip 43: Love Game

Looking for some new friends?

Arrange for multiple matches to meet your attractive opposite-sex alter-ego at the same place and time. Show up and claim that you have been tricked just like everyone else.

Bond over drinks and the shared experience!

Tip 44: Bait and Switch

Hoping to boost your online dating prospects?

Create a good-looking Tinder alter-ego. Remain inactive for a week and let the right swipes roll in.

After a week, update your profile with your real photos and swipe right at the profiles that you like.

Tip 45: Tidying Up with Catfishing

Fed up with your dirty roommate?

Create an attractive fake Tinder profile and match with him or her. Then say that you'll be coming over to the apartment for your first date.

Sit back and watch the long-awaited cleaning process commence.

Tip 46: Dine and Ghost

Need to drive traffic to your restaurant or café?

Set up a few Tinder dates at said location with the help of an attractive profile. Tell your match that you'll be late and ask him or her to order something expensive for you.

Once the dish is served, tell your match you can't make it after all.

Note: Soften the blow with excuses like "an emergency!" or "I think you're really hot but my boyfriend/girlfriend found out about this date". You don't want your match to associate your restaurant with bad memories.

Section 4: Life Hacks

Tip 47: Borrowed Time

Unable to finish a paper in time for the deadline?

Submit a paper that you have completed for another class on time. It will take some time before your professor realizes that you've submitted the wrong paper.

Use the interval period to finish your paper.

Tip 48: Wi-Fi Speed Hack

Can't get your family or roommates to agree to split the costs on upgrading your internet speed?

Adjust the router admin settings to ensure that their go-to devices have the lowest bandwidths.

When the complaints start coming, tell them that the only option is to upgrade to a faster plan.

Tip 49: Keyboard Warrior

Want to win an internet argument easily?

Edit your comments after your opponent has responded.

It will appear as if he or she has no clue of what the debate is about.

Tip 50: Undetectable

Wanted to get away with cheating on an important examination?

Teach yourself Braille and use it to create a cheat sheet.

Place the sheet in your hoodie so that you can access the answers without even looking at it – just "read" the answers with your non-dominant hand.

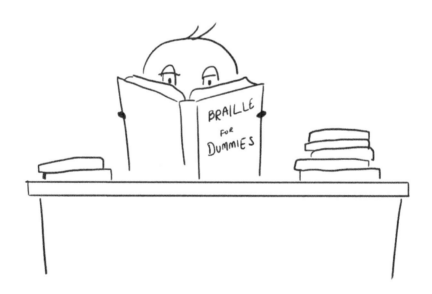

Tip 51: Bad Liar

Want to get better at lying?

Instead of trying to seem like you're telling the truth, make it painfully obvious that you're lying.

When you actually need to lie about something, people will be more likely to believe that you're telling the truth.

Note: You can include an embarrassing detail to make your lie more convincing.

Tip 52: Doing the Dishes

Want to get out of a tedious household chore?

Take some clean plates and wet them. Then put them in the drying rack.

Tell your spouse or roommate that you've washed your "half" of the dishes.

Tip 53: Tactful Exclusion

Don't want to directly exclude some annoying friends or acquaintances from your social plans?

Make sure that your next event takes place when they can't go.

You can then invite them with the knowledge that they will have to turn you down.

Tip 54: Off the Streets

Want to reduce the number of homeless people in your area?

Give them some fake money.

They might get arrested and imprisoned, effectively keeping them off the streets.

Tip 55: Smart Driving

Can't find a way to cut into another lane of traffic?

Wait for a Tesla to appear and cut in front of it.

The autopilot feature will force it to brake. Mission accomplished.

Tip 56: Anti-Spamming Measures

Don't want to put up with spam calls from a scam company anymore?

Go to the company's website and give them your local congressman's office phone number.

Chances are that the influx of spam calls will prompt them to take effective action.

Tip 57: Good Housekeeping

Want to make the most of your new housekeeper's services?

Put in the effort to clean your home to the best of your ability right before she arrives.

She can then focus her efforts on the big things (e.g. removing shower grout) rather than the little things that you can easily handle yourself.

Tip 58: Acquaintances with Benefits

Hoping for some extra wedding presents?

Look up the mailing addresses of known billionaires and send each of them a wedding invite.

Their secretary might simply send you a gift without confirming if their busy boss actually knows who you are.

Tip 59: The Homeless Problem

Concerned about the number of homeless people in your town?

Donate to the homeless shelters in a neighboring town instead.

Watch the homeless slowly migrate away to the next town.

Tip 60: Who Let the Dogs Out?

Sick of cleaning up the dog poop from your lawn?

Put up a warning about the use of toxic pesticides on your lawn.

Dog owners who see it will keep their dog far, far away.

Tip 61: Stop Telemarketing Me

Sick of getting harassed by telemarketers all day?

Give them a taste of their own medicine by sexually harassing them over the phone.

If you're convincing enough, they will eventually block your number from their database.

Tip 62: Reckless Driving

Worried about all the reckless drivers in your neighborhood?

Place a large photograph of a child and some flowers on the side of the road.

This should prompt those who see it to drive more carefully.

Tip 63: How Good Liars are Made

Want your children to excel at the art of lying?

Overreact towards everything they do as they grow up.

They will inevitably learn how to twist the truth when necessary.

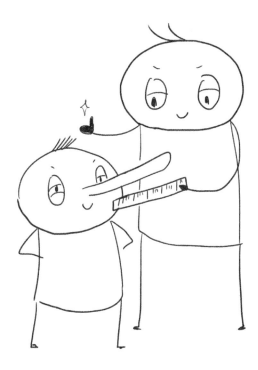

Tip 64: Truth Detector

Want to know when your child is pretending to sleep?

Make it a point to tell them that they snore loudly in their sleep.

When you hear them snoring, you'll know that they are faking it.

Tip 65: Fat Shaming

Tired of being put down for your weight?

Tell the next person who calls you fat that you used to be 75 pounds heavier.

They will look and feel like the asshole that they are.

Tip 66: Travel Insurance

Want to ensure that there's a win-win situation in the event that your airlines loses your luggage?

As you pack, take photos of large amounts of cash in your luggage.

You can then claim that the airline owes you a large amount of money in the event that they misplace your luggage.

Tip 67: Airplane Etiquette

Is the person sitting in front of you on a flight reclining his or her seat into your personal space?

Direct the air conditioning above you towards the top of their head and turn it on to full blast.

They will eventually readjust their seat position and leave your personal space intact.

Tip 68: Secondary Security Screening Selection

Did the airlines desk just hand you a boarding pass with the dreaded SSSS?

Throw it away and use the boarding pass on your phone instead.

Display your digital boarding pass to TSA at the gate. Bon voyage!

Note: This only works if you also checked in online and if you are not on the permanent SSSS list.

Tip 69: Ethical Impersonation

Need to create fake online profile?

Instead of appropriating someone else's photos, use www.thispersondoesnotexist.com to generate an AI-made composite face.

Now you'll never have to worry about getting called out for impersonating someone else.

Tip 70: The Kindness of Strangers

Hoping to get some money from strangers at a gas station?

Instead of asking them for cash, tell them that you need a small amount of money for gas to make it home.

Thank them for their sympathy and enjoy their generosity.

Tip 71: Kids-Free Dining

Found a restaurant that you would like to frequent?

Label it as being "unfriendly for kids" on Google Reviews or Yelp.

Chances are that there will be fewer kids around to annoy you the next time you dine there.

Tip 72: Social Drug Use

Looking for some free pot?

Go on Craigslist and look for accommodations for rent that are specifically looking for "420 friendly" roommates? Make an appointment to view the place.

You will probably be invited to smoke up with the existing tenants to test your social compatibility. Enjoy the free weed and some (hopefully) good company.

Tip 73: Knock Knock

Did you just hear an unexpected knock on your door?

Assuming that you don't have a peephole, the best thing to do is to answer it with a kettle of boiling hot water.

Use it as a weapon or a gesture of hospitality depending on who's there.

Tip 74: Trespasser

Interested in getting into a gated community without the security code?

Use 9911. This is often used as a backup code for emergency personnel to enter.

Tip 75: Trespasser's Alibi

Worried about getting caught for trespassing?

Bring along a dog leash.

If the property owner confronts you, just tell him or her that your dog escaped.

Tip 76: Adoption

Thinking of adopting a child and concerned that he or she might be bullied for being adopted?

Teach them to respond to bullying with "At least I am sure that my adoptive parents wanted me. Your parents probably had you by mistake."

Parenting is easier when you don't have to worry about bullies.

Tip 77: Riding Dirty

Feeling anxious about driving in the presence of a policeman when you have drugs in your car?

Pick your nose.

Your body language will signal that you're oblivious and carefree – the polar opposite of the guilty, anxious and paranoid suspect the cops have been trained to look out for.

Tip 78: Silly Boy

Worried that a drug dog might smell out your stash?

Make your edibles resemble dog treats.

If you're found out, the dog's handler will assume that it was attracted to the treats.

Tip 79: Anti-Vaxxers

Are you worried that unvaccinated children might spread an infectious disease to your child?

Spread rumors that unvaccinated children can become autistic via exposure to vaccinated children.

Let them form their own segregated community and infect each other with vaccine-preventable diseases.

Section 5:
All is Fair in Love and War

Tip 80: Blood Suckers

Did you just hear a mosquito buzzing in your bedroom at night?

Hide under the covers while exposing some of your partner's flesh.

Lie low until the mosquitoes have had their fill.

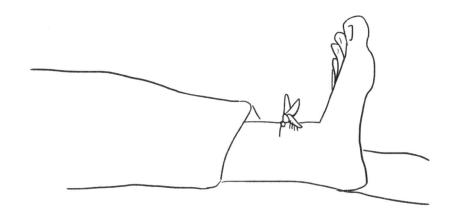

Tip 81: Risk Management

Tempted to cheat on your spouse?

If yes, be sure to cheat with someone who is also married (it is even better if there are also children to consider).

Since they also have much to lose, you'll be better positioned to keep the affair secret.

Tip 82: Olfactory Camouflage

Worried that your wife might find out about your infidelity?

Give your wife and your mistress the same perfume.

Your wife's sense of smell is less likely to alert her to what's going on.

Tip 83: Diaper Duty

Want to get out of parenting's most disgusting obligation?

Make a big show out of smelling your baby's (still unsoiled) diaper and pretending to change it in the next room.

The next time the diaper actually needs to be changed, you can claim that it's not your turn since you were the one who previously changed it.

Tip 84: Getting Along

Are you tired of dealing with your girlfriend or wife's annoying female friend?

Casually reveal that you consider her to be attractive or good looking.

Your partner will be less likely to make plans that include all three of you in the future.

Tip 85: The Naughty List

Want to order things online that require discretion while living with a spouse or family members?

Do so right before Christmas.

If they spot the package in question, tell them that its contents are off-limits because it's a Christmas gift.

Tip 86: Caller ID

Worried that your spouse will find out about your affair through your phone?

Change your lover's saved name to "Scam Likely".

You now have an alibi for all the calls that might arouse suspicion.

MESSAGES   NOW

Scam Likely

PHONE   5m ago

Scam Likely
Missed Call (3)

MESSAGES   10m ago

Scam Likely
Where ru

MESSAGES   1h ago

Scam Likely

Tip 87: Lawyering Up

Are you planning to initiate a divorce?

Arrange a consultation with all the top divorce attorneys in your area without your spouse's knowledge.

When it's time for your spouse to hire an attorney, all of them will deem themselves to be biased for having met with you first.

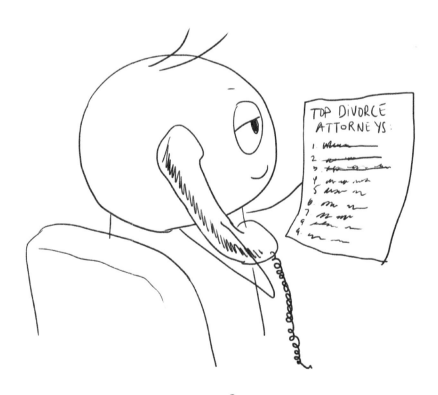

Section 6:
Profit Maximization

99

Section 6:
Profit Maximization

Tip 88: Free Coffee

Do you want free coffee from a popular chain?

Register 365 accounts on the popular chain's website or app. Each account should have a different birthday.

Enjoy your birthday reward (free coffee) every day of the year.

Tip 89: Yard Sale Advertising

Want to attract more passersby to your yard sale?

Place all the most attractive items that you don't actually want to sell front and center. Then attach some tags to indicate that all of them have been sold.

Those who come over to inspect them will probably take the time to browse all the stuff that you actually want to sell.

Tip 90: Designated Beneficiaries

Are you interested in a long term means of financial gain?

Approach your close friends and tell them that you made them a beneficiary of your partial life insurance plan.

They will feel obliged to do the same. You can expect a windfall if any of them dies before you.

Note: They may kill you.

Tip 91: Foot Traffic

Do you want to boost sales at your coffee shop?

Set off the fire alarm in nearby office buildings.

Rack up additional sales from all the temporarily displaced employees.

Tip 92: Gold Digging

Are you a college student with hopes of finding a rich boyfriend or girlfriend?

Look up your college's list of Top Parental Donors. Find out who their children are and seduce the best match.

Enjoy the spoils.

Tip 93: Insurance Fraud

Frustrated that your postal service keeps losing your mail?

Insure your mail. Then send yourself letters on a frequent basis.

You will now make money whenever one of your fake letters gets lost.

Tip 94: Written Off

Do you have a rich and racist grandparent?

Present him or her with a Photoshopped picture of your sibling getting married to a black spouse.

You'll end up with a larger share of the inheritance once your sibling is written out of the will.

Tip 95: Flat Tires

Do you want to drive sales to your bicycle shop?

Scatter a bunch of glass fragments near your shop (discreetly).

You'll get more business when cyclists eventually puncture their tires as they approach your place.

Note: The same tip applies for auto tire repairs and nails.

Tip 96: Halo Effect

Thinking of selling your car?

Be sure to take photographs of your vehicle in an upscale neighborhood.

Prospective buyers will assume that you've had the resources to keep it well maintained. They will be likelier to offer you a higher price.

Note: This can also work for houses but in the opposite way. Simply leave a few junk cars parked around a house you are trying to buy for cheap.

Tip 97: Food Delivery

Want to make some money off apps like Postmates, DoorDash or UberEats?

Make your orders in the early hours of the morning (e.g. 4 am).

You might receive some extra credit or vouchers when there's no drivers around to deliver your order.

Tip 98: Fireproof

Want to claim more insurance money in the event that your house goes up in flames?

Buy (or borrow) a large number of expensive items and place them in prominent locations. Use a video camera to record everything in your home afterwards.

Note: You could also just return all the items to the store once you're done and are sure that your footage is secured. Instead of worrying about property damage, you'll be looking forward to it.

Tip 99: Business Proposition

Thinking of how to get back from a bankruptcy or a financially disadvantageous situation?

Relocate to a small town and become a locksmith. After it gets dark, go around and lock all the car doors you can (rural folk often leave their car doors unlocked).

Enjoy the inflated demand for your services the next day.

Tip 100: Pixelated

Planning to rob a bank?

Be sure to hold your middle finger in front of your face while you do it.

When a news channel broadcasts the bank's security footage, they will be forced to blur your face along with your finger.

Tip 101: Publishing Strategy

Want to write a reasonably successful book but don't have any original insights?

Appropriate the most popular posts from a broadly relevant subreddit and fashion the content into an attractive book.

Sell the book while acknowledging its source of inspiration.

Special thanks to the following Reddit Users:

u/Neckbeard_Police	u/snoof123
u/thepianokeynecktie	u/Western_You
u/smallchimpu	u/TheStorkClipper
u/sahie	u/ekvin0
u/AudaxProtinus	u/socialist111
u/mrmojofilter	u/BudgetJellyfish
u/AvianLawman	u/skinjelly
u/reddituser123988	u/tarandfeathers
u/Tjetom	u/depthandbloom
u/mannyosu	u/Coccyx_Avenger
u/Sylocule	u/FantasyMaster85
u/bluejellybeans0711	u/jakk86
u/mcgonagallstwin	u/b_random9
u/mozgarob	u/Macluawn
u/ChaoticFather	u/fig-lebowski
u/cannabisqueenkitty	u/OmarFromtheWire2
u/abeannis	u/SarcasticCroissant
u/zook420	u/MedievilMusician
u/cbildfell	u/AnonUserAccount
u/Onywan	u/Rainmert
u/pac_man2321	u/Skydiever
u/PoppaPickle	u/Royal-Derpness
u/The-Real-Mario	u/SouthDistribution
u/shookron	u/CharltonBreezy
u/mahniij	u/lightandvariable
u/sotheg8r	u/tylerdurden1993
u/midwrestless	u/skydiverbrent
u/rayjensen	u/gottalovefacts
u/Dasw0n	u/growleroz
u/AlexWasTakenWasTaken	u/brockm92
u/vortexbeater	u/El_Duderino1980
u/almostbobsaget	u/changleosingha
u/A-ladder-named-chaos	u/existentialzebra
u/BlackCoke2	u/Disastrous_Plankton
u/mrthatsthat	u/RoguishPrince
u/MasterDealer	u/pinkgandhi
u/Captain_Ahbvious	u/acvdk
u/InJpnHrtSrgn1StdyHnd	u/DildosB4BrosB4Hoes
u/itherm	u/Zuke020
u/gingerbhoy	u/realmenus
u/Mango_Punch	u/MiniJose
u/actually_crazy_irl	u/Anyonegotacookie
u/HronkChaos	u/Sockemslol2
u/Aoozzz	u/Lightningbolt724
u/puzzydestroyer69	u/newthingsforus
u/NUTS_STUCK_TO_LEG	u/PM_ME_GIBSONS
u/Daanoking	u/Life_God_Lemonade
u/The2500	u/windirfull
	u/LeviathanGray

Printed in Great Britain
by Amazon

32863757R00069